Coloring Book

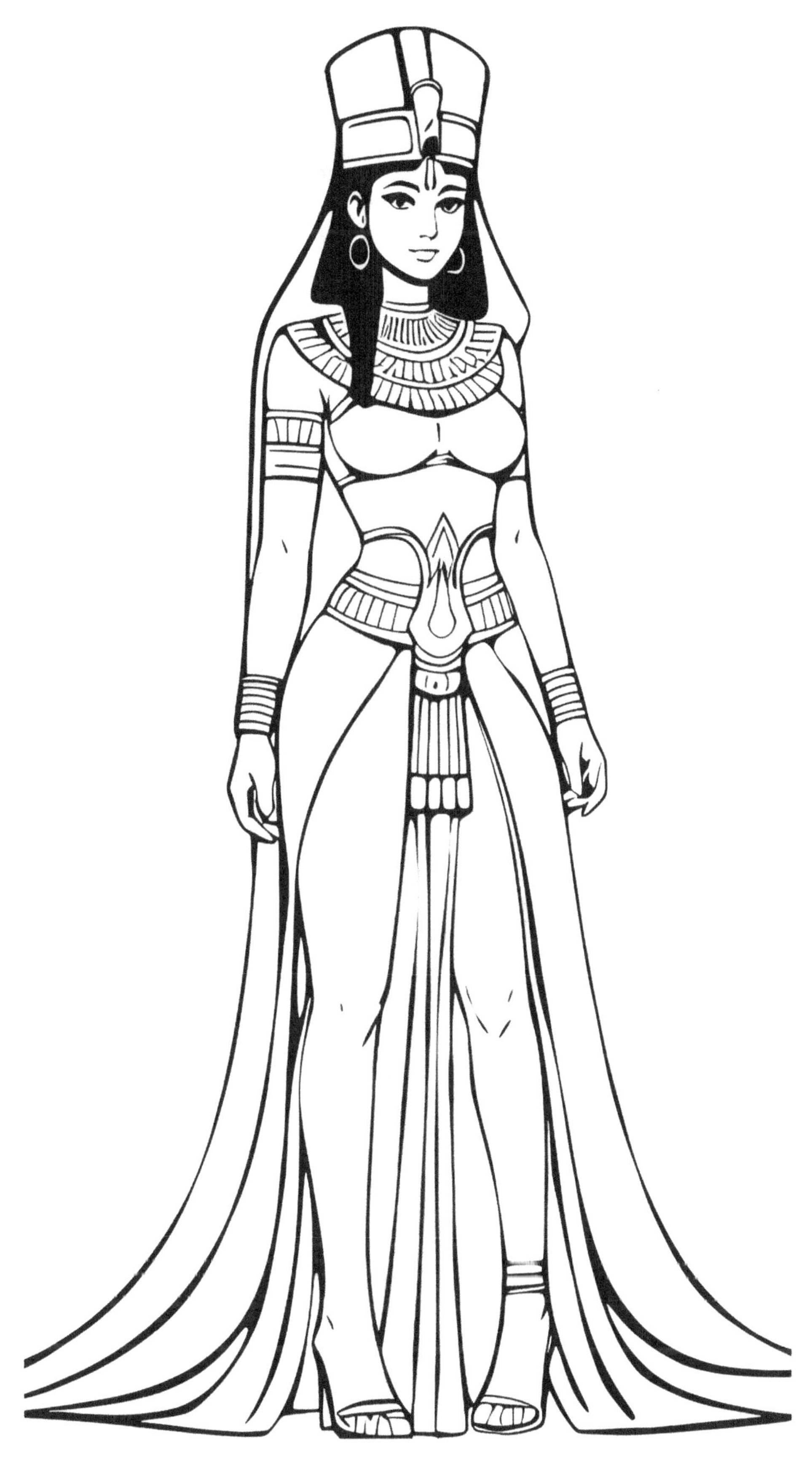

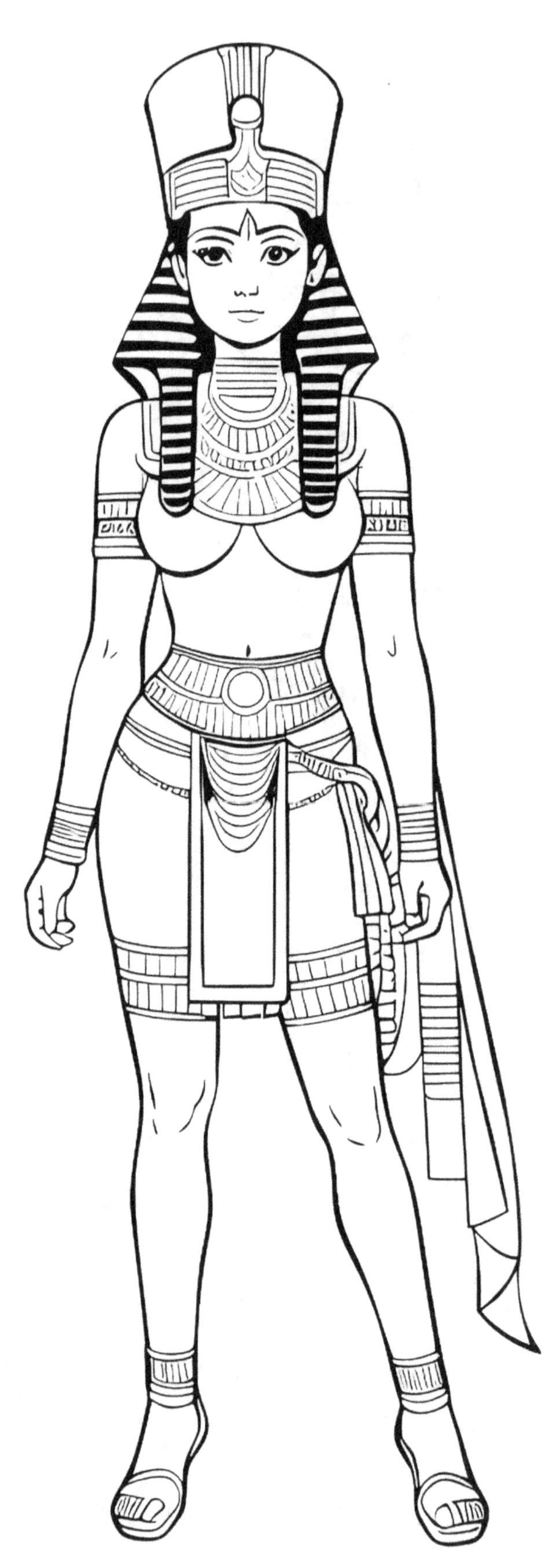

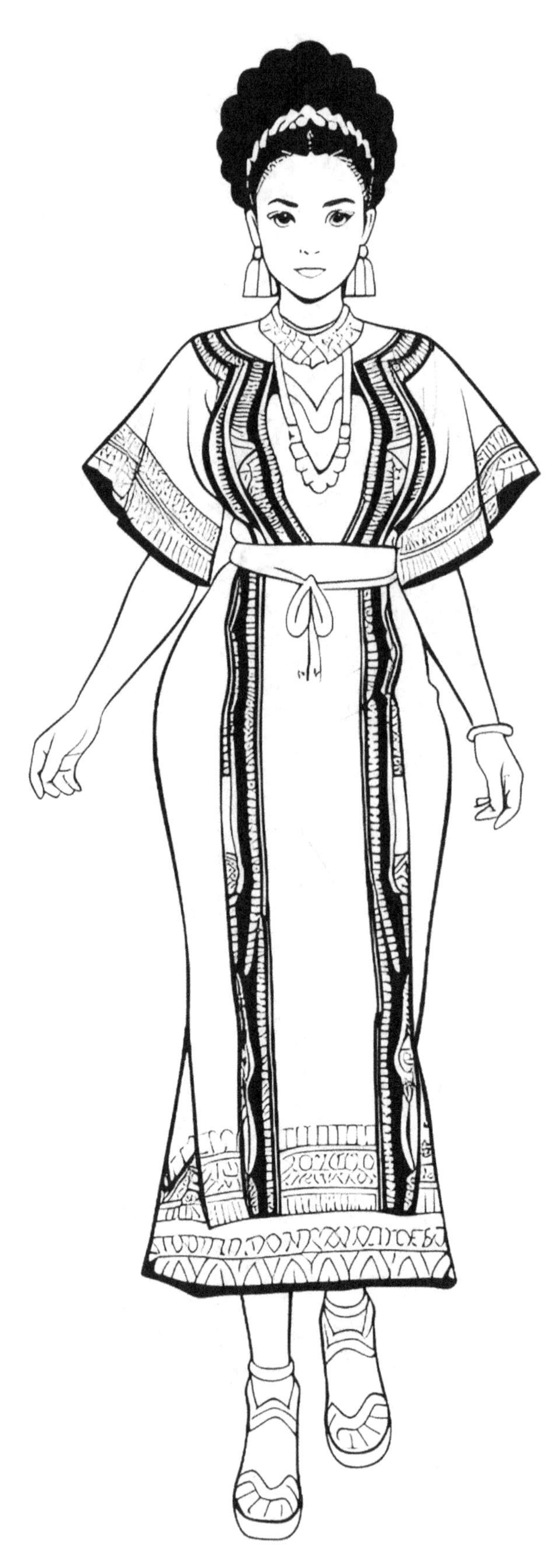

A Heartfelt Thank You

Dear Valued Buyer,
we want to extend our deepest gratitude for choosing to embark on this
colorful journey with us. Your support and appreciation mean the
world to us, and we're thrilled that our creations found a place in your
world of imagination.
We hope these pages have brought you joy, relaxation, and
endless inspiration. Your artistic touch has transformed these designs
into vibrant works of art, and we couldn't be more
grateful for your creativity.
Thank you for being a part of our coloring book community. We look
forward to sharing morc colorful adventures with you in the future.
With heartfelt thanks,

IMAGINOVIA CREATIONS